PAPER MOONS

NATALIA PROKOPOWICZ

Published by Natalia Prokopowicz

ISBN: 978-1-7635049-1-2 (paperback)
ISBN: 978-1-7635049-0-5 (hardcover)

First edition, 2024

For book orders and enquiries,
contact: nprokopowicz85@gmail.com

NATIONAL LIBRARY OF AUSTRALIA

A catalogue record for this book is available from the National Library of Australia

To my inner child;
I dedicate this to her
and to those who
find salvation in my poetry.
I hear you.

CONTENTS

HE AND SHE

He's convoluted as if poison, hidden bare through her veins
she's like the air, carrying the weight that the sound of silent
waves create.

He failed a meaningful and curious watch
she drew hearts on her left wrist, hoping secretly he'd trace
them.

He played bank, called house, gambled gold
she held tighter, kept fighting, like the colours of the
dragonfly that hang from the dash
lowly.

He solidified on tarnished ground what he'd swear to her,
to apologise for promises
he promised he'd keep.
She counted hours, drove round the blue mailbox
final tears of restless stillness.

He knew he tasted sweet, quite like a holey apple, one bite
assisted by traditional meetings.
She followed effortlessly true, to keep up with the runaway,
loving the part of him that he considered damaged goods.

He saw an opportunity to take common greed, in some way
he's troubled, sorry, bleeding.
She empathized, carried and yearned for more,
because eyes tell stories
and his are beautifully flawed.

LIVE VICARIOUSLY

You know where to find me,
amid the music.

Peeks encapsulate an epiphany, crystallising a single grit
in blackout, I grasp futile hopes, words adrift
on indifference's sunken ravine.

I swore I wouldn't hold out hope and pretend
if you didn't bless the river water I left running in my
Alaska.

My ravenous love is so supple it's delicate
it wouldn't do to turn my back on it.
I mustn't suckle the wound,

the most normal one.

I just can't change
or be any less than I am.

YOU FELL IN LOVE WITH THE IDEA OF ME

I forgot what we talked about in those days.
Only I recall the moments I felt you close
every move was a step nearer towards me.
I willed you to want me so badly,
that I'd wondered too long if you were indifferent
after you left.
Saying I was it, you lavished about that good feeling.
Locking me in with the keychain you gifted me
our inside joke until you shut me out.
But the flirting was more, the kisses meant something
different.
Your hands told lies and I chose to see through their truth
once you decided I was too good for you.
I stopped doing the things I'd usually do.
I swear I almost changed a bit after you.
And I remember how after that first week I couldn't even
cry anymore, that I felt something heavier inside.
Your voice and your face
every time I thought I could look at you, you had me to die.
This road is so long because you carry yourself
along my mind.
I wish I didn't feel the need to chase you up.
Because you scorned my heart and hurt it when you weren't
careful, so it's up to me to mend your carelessness.
In which I wanted you badly, I wanted you to want me
and everyone to want me,
more than anything in the whole entire world.
And you wonder why I've been the way I have.
It's because of you, everything comes back to you.

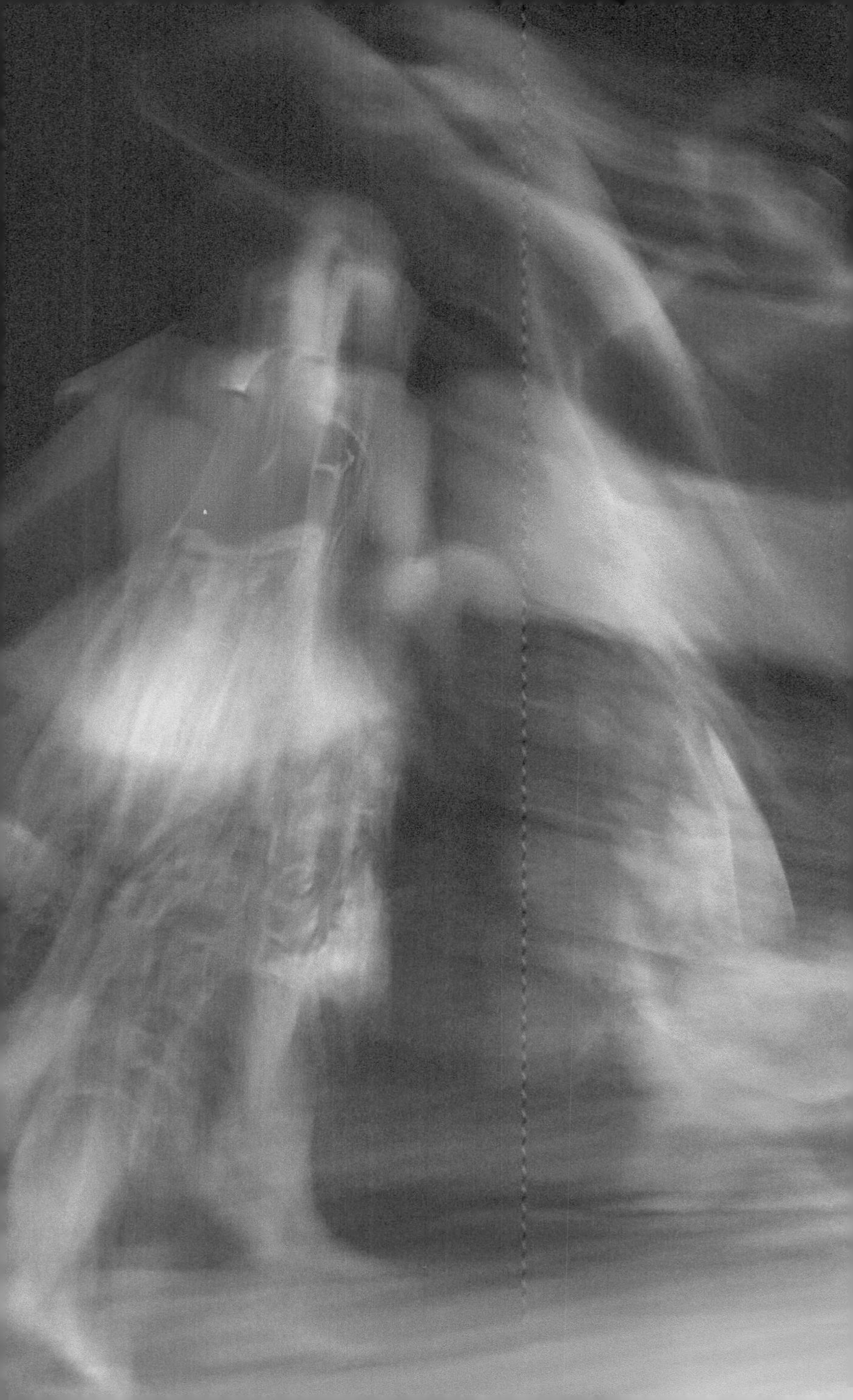

CURSED

I think it's true our family is cursed
and those who abandon us are lucky to get out alive.

And maybe our kind of sideways love would find its place in some other time,
but I don't want to think that given the chance
I might run back to him.

Because we get how that works
and from the last guy, I trace the same scars.

So to keep you off my mind
I think of you like I don't think of you,
in distractions,
in my bed.
With my cat's
floating about in my head.

When you fell like a hazy on me,
but you lied.

And it occurred to me
when I lost my lucky on the very first day of school.

ALL OR NOTHING, RIGHT?

I was dear in my agonies
I took place in the white ghost on potent nights.

And I courier about your omniscient smile
regal,
right into the devil's advocacy.

Your embrace introduced me to loss of sleep.
Anger in my above.
An insecure inconsistency
in which I need to remember the parts you didn't take up.

I knew to be weary of you
but I laid my eggs too soon
as you had, when you walked into the room.

Calling my name
this was you leaving me, worried and consumed.

My hurt felt like paper cuts
unseen, but they stung.

Doing me right by wrong.
I couldn't help but think your absence left my future
somewhat uncertain,
in my very own home.

APPLE TO THE EYE

Wounded warrior in the untouched corners
of my single bed
I reach there sometimes.

Overly critical or analytical maybe not,
but to myself that I could be.

With the broken shoes
I leave here where I stay.
Waiting at the back door step
to sabotage and be bitter.
To like you and spite you the closer
the next.

Something a little different
something created inside
from the dictators in my life,
which I'm left with no surprise.

Raving on about new conceptions
where I see both sides of the story.

I could,
or I could choose not to.
Be pounced on from the swords at my stand
or be proud to be different.

AT HOW I'M LOOKING AT LOVE

At how I'm looking at love
look at how it would find me now.
The avalanche I see in its hit
the wait for closer contact for the phone to never ring.

And the pirates linger by the deadline
something stronger than cigarettes and alkaline.

Soon it's known that the ones you once loved were
temporary
your friends hadn't cared a bit because they didn't have to.

Standing in the gallows
whips lashing at my body.

Looking away love looked at me,
setting me free with the worst mailed out
deceased.

BETTER TO FEEL THAN NOT

Second choice

allowing my hand to run alone along this wall again.
Because I had courage and kindness
I had been something you couldn't feel at the time.
Every professor that went by
was a woman on her bike telling you that you had life.
Listening in plentiful blank beds of roses
I'd stay for hours while you worked.

Every scent you left me to find
going to lengths and together we'd climb.

I learnt how warm and how good a boy could feel
you cared so quietly but my pain was filled.
Showing me how absent and detached you could be
it was us against the pattern you needed.

And I loved you with my heart and my soul but my mind
I couldn't decide without your help
because you left me behind.

I collapsed and I cried and I could've laughed at how small
you were,
but I saw potential in that glaze of yours.
I cleaned you out and rested well
our karma maybe once maybe not complete.

But I cannot excuse you only forgive
I only dismiss what a chance you missed.

BLUE LILY

Does your tongue taste like red raspberry?
I imagine it tastes like black liquorish warm and icy.

But by the lick of any other gun could be so bitter sweet
mismatched by the eye with tools out the ready.

Sinister to look at again and remember what was once there.
Making my hands dirty when they were drunken with
impulse.

With these cheap themes painted to unfit
I made myself and I see only it.

Lethargic in an absence of true loveliness
falling to pieces waiting for my kiss.

BROTHER'S CRY

A snapped wing brews at the beetle's mend

hemlock and venom.

Today I drive slow,
because I know my behaviour can change many things.
An eagles dream that pet's me softly
in the dark of a closet
I once felt safe.

Mundane, a fellow corpse
I the Parisian cat.

And mother always put our ironed clothes on warm
giddish and giggly.

CHRONIC

That was I
thrown out with the glass and paper.
Inevitable and unlit.
Foiled in conscientiousness, too full, the bucket.
To fill a pail
that smells like spearmint and deep sleep.

It feels like I can't do it anymore.
I touch wood.
I can hear screaming
and fighting, and words that don't know how to be said.
And all I can see is confusion and bear tolerance
border genius, that forces me to beat it.

Narrow it down
simplify it.
It there's something wrong with me, I forget.

I wasn't the white swan
I am the wolf who passes the treaty line,
trailing the broken bones longing to fix dangers.

Captains orders.

COUNTRY ROADS

Tall tales burnt into silos, on those country roads
I can still imagine them.
How the meadows smell and breathe with gushes of
freedom.

When you are supplied with that kind of magic
that electricity
things are different.

So at one point my palms stopped sweating
before the coffee turned bitter, my secrets were addressed.
Months allowed me to be alright
they were quiet but I listened.

After the sun turned golden one thousand times each night
I stopped dying every time I was lectured for being too
young, for never being old enough.

My ancestors were told by there's
generations of pride and family curses.

I didn't need it because I wasn't the problem.
It was people's wounds, reflected in their own selves
and capacity to love,
not their ego.

So they could never reach me
as I them.
I untangled the roots after all.
My trees' thankful to be watered.

CRADLES LUCK

Soak it up my cradles luck
dinner starts at five.
Two stones but only one bird
it took more than that to kill a man
I heard.

And you're indifferent you swear it
I see it in your eyes.
It's not enough
the first thing on the shelf
so reach for the back and hope that the best thing is hidden
do tell.

You'll always agree, I know it's scary.
That the one thing that's going good can be contrary.

But promise your promises something.
No matter how the bargain
you can't agree for less.

FORGET ME

The watcher, the shrill on the cliff ledge.
The urge to fall off when I can barely stand.

And I know this much
I am young, to not worry about a thing.
To be a good little girl
lack of validation
lack of anything.

My lonely hour is from eight to twelve.
Where my roses need watering
when my heart starts to swell.
Where the light in my life doesn't get enough sun.
One way ticket to Saturn
Venus
maybe Pluto.

Where does my youth go?

Why can't I feed it?

FRAUD

Fraud
rowing upon your midnight lake roots.

The leaves playing as if they remember their existence
before they fell.
I can only imagine it with somebody else.

You'd have fit neatly in my jean pocket
imperfectly perfect in the way your thumb grazed my jaw.

I thought I knew it well
your strange yet familiar smell.

Like how creatures play and hunt in the night
it reminded you of your real identity
that I'd have to forfeit because it wasn't right.

I needed to find clues

champagne

I fancied you.

You had too,
but it was too good to be true.

Love bombs
ghost trails I wished I could leave them behind.
But you set me up to fail, in this flawed image of you
blurry and blue.

I STILL LISTEN

If you cried me a river I think I'd still listen
once you play by the rules I'd still play with you.

Because I know you cheated them and I know I let you
perhaps I could ask you why?

It's not on me anymore
will you take initiative?

Will you do what's right?

But I don't think it's bothering you at night.

I think you're hiding in plain sight
and I think that's alright.

JUST A BOY

I shouldn't I know
because you're not worth much and you're slow.

I don't because you're small.

You don't understand and now I write about you.

I can't because you do no tell.
You take me for granted and you hurt as well.

I take your hand but you drop it off
down at the debt, where we don't go anymore.
You smile right by me
I smile back

there are no words to answer that.

What do you want from me
what can you give me?

Are there things you're dying to tell me
things that you are not?

There is nothing about you accept how you make me feel.

I couldn't waste my time unless you were willing.

I let you go because you're just a boy.

KEEP IT TO YOURSELF OR FIND ME

Forever can be just a second as my forever belongs to me
just as I gifted thorns to my flower.
Announcing that sometimes my silence is just exhaustion
yearning in her gentle reminder.

Because I won't stop until I'm proud.

I'm prouder than somebody's dream girl.

Letting go to see what stayed was worth my cage

ghosts just as lonely as me until I am free.

LACED FRAGRANCE IN MY BEDROOM

You must be laced with pomegranate in order to have pity.

Chambered wickedness that proposes Winter.
And bloom a promise with drips of sweeter spice
your shallowness
kept at my kind.

When in life I've been treated like a child
in tempered youth I am.

But in bravery, in having more

I am a mystery
drawn complete.

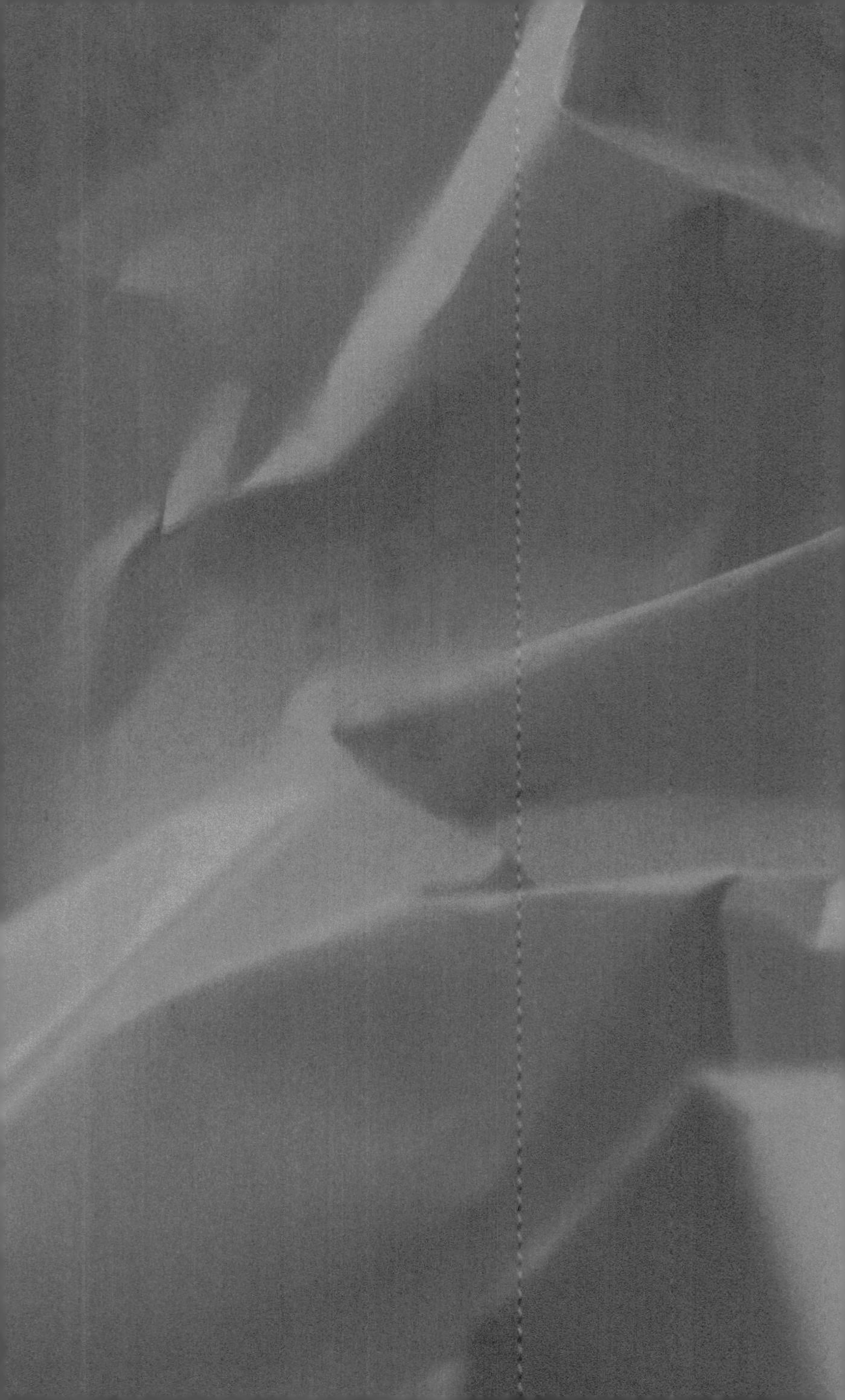

LITTLE LION

Come on little lion
it seems that you were never here.
And yet it seems that all is left is an essence of a letter to descript your efforts
and yet your efforts could not be enough for that set by curriculum.

It seems all that's left is the essence of a woman too grand
to be tall enough.
Too grand that she had been listened to by no one
and no one at all.

A world so childish and ignorant.
A world so good that all had to be hidden.

Who will love you after you yourself are gone?
Who will smile when you yourself are not even there.

Because you are more than ready
you're ready whenever they are.

Don't give me up

don't give it up.

What about life and what about growing old and kinder
what about being experienced and fulfilled?

Fulfillment has always been in the little things
it is rather difficult to even come close to the end.

MELODY OF A BABE

Death haunted me nightly little.

Now every ghost I know has been my vigilance.

And so I really enjoy when the road is soaked

It's dark but I'm not cold because I'm the only one watching
this show.

I know I start to become my own figment of imagination
I don't remember my hours before as I used to.

I think I'm clouded by my own clouds
my sun is hidden a bit there.

To be vocal about my figure
they're figure is vocal
as had once been about mine.

The calm before the storm.

That of which I will probably be made blind to.

LOVE LIKE HER

Would you listen or would you talk?

Hurt at the heart by concrete stars and pavement.

You'd prefer me in lost disposition in some galaxy in my head
because on ground I slip away in the world.

And I found refuge in the longest time
wondering about explorers who discovered their heath.

My cuffed antler wings,
flowered of thorns, smelling of roses
bitten to perfection.
Be told small earthquakes
I feel coming
faint.

I wanted to show everyone my map of the world's.
I was too faded, long lost bedtime stories told in the dark.
Sleeping in the side wing
the right wing
taking freeway exists that left me again.

MEDICINE

I sip your medicine
a non-relief to these drugs.
The system isn't working
not even you my love.

There's a cliff over there where your heart stands.
Over here I can bear you but I can't get to know you.
I'll kiss your cheek and supplement the need for hands.
Don't stand in my way because I keep giving you chances.

I stand better to let you lead.
You come in stronger to understand the mysterious dances.
Darling I keep holding
you unfold and as soon as it's done you discoed.

Walk past me as I catch up to smell that's black mold
are you a disease that I accept my time to keep?

Flinching is your desire but truly you warm up to me.
Unexpectedly you grab my hand,
but it's just a dream going too deep.

Undecided,
petrified your eyes.
Come closer
I'm open prided.

But you stare with confusion and web up those lies.

MY CONDOLENCES

My condolences
I puppy eye your losses.

Fraud by daylight
hot shot on lamp light.

Your expenses paid at my cost
secret rich writing you out.

Collapse
even the kite of time.

Drop it low
drop it silent.

Play it again
as if it's never been heard before.

MY CRIMES

My crimes to want such things
innocence at my behalf but it's screaming for battle.

Expectations are what deceased me
insurrection of perfection

that I am not right.

Nobody can ask more of you
to find you as righteous because of your gender.

That eyes can only see beyond the soul
not even so.

My key word doesn't exit
it's time to exit this abyss.

PILLS

You finally came home.

Reeking of third day wash and wasted spirit.
Yesterday's breakfast was your weekends mistake.
Burdened upon others
spewing what's left of it in the laundry sink.
Spilling about not only the contents of booze and brains
but doors and bed sheets too.
Crushing your fingers and cursing at those who actually
love you.

While consumed in your own sorrow and regret.
You neglect the responsibility of being a brother
an un-clear picture of yourself in the mirror.

Burnt in the fires of your strength long before
missed opportunities to say sorry.
Which you wrestled against when I told you I didn't want
to speak to you
where you shut the door like a man child.

Liver deadline cut
coughing fit in your kennel cave.
I hear it from your bedroom
the noises I never expected you to make.
You lift a veil of actions that breeds to hurt others
feeling like words can start to trigger loss of breath
repetition is missed.
Smelling fumes of things you don't want to talk about
that you won't take it anywhere
but you'll deal with it all over this sombre house.

POL

REVENGE

He smudges it.
Smudges the black ink written in the wince of the paper
thin walls.
Gurgling his fist at the words he couldn't find upon a child's
ushering cry.
Biting at the eyes so tired for the chance
to survive.

Sitting at the table in front of his wife who has to hide his
method of survival.
Crossing her arms around her head as he struggles to
straighten his march towards the only person
to blame.
That other than the mirror which can't say much
other than the memories which he can't sacrifice not to touch.

Dusting the pavement he never longed to chance
until the day his son was taken from him
on the notorious early morning hour.

Serpentine a gun he shed at the jury
paralysed from
default
depression
loneliness.

What was his life if only this?

The hollow, the empty, the unforgiving gut punching mess.
Shallow pupils in the comfort of his builders hands
the language of his youth, the disconnect he needed to lose.

RONALD

I look at you and I don't see any of us
I never could.

I wish I knew you the way I felt I should
it's much too dark.

Darker for you when your body was preparing itself for the
moment
you knew.

But you caught up at the right time
the wrong mindset although.

Because how might you miss someone you never met?

I cherish your mind.

I only wish I could see you too
your soul.

Is it in me
or are you everywhere now?

RUM ON MY ROSES

Rum on my roses,

stake in my fall.

Moss on the roots,

mistaken my call.

Sun peeking through various tips,

certain smells that hold strength.

Adventure for two feet,

not a sound in sight.

Liquid flushing atop fingers,

mellowness of the voice.

Crows and ravens dancing to ballroom works,

kissing the cold that no longer wants touch.

SABOTAGER, I MADE THE EVER FLAME

It wasn't a moment when you kissed me
it was just accomplished.
As we held each other in the cold
in the rain.
Teeth and lips brushing
my realest yet.
The simplest form of everything.
The same day you promised me with a gentle safety
you also gave me up.
Not me, not my style, not the best you had
but you got rid of you.
Like I was a hard drug
a piece of clothing you bought, liked, and wore out.
We call it fast fashion
you call it sabotage.
How can I write about you when in the end you gifted me
with confusion?
Time.
Because my peculiar heart melted like sweet butter
my eyes searched greater ways to want to paint you.
And you held me like you were in love with me
like I was all you ever wanted, what you said to me
what you knew, a muse.
It's as if the stories half done
as if I couldn't write for weeks.
That I stood far away
like how my dignity told me I deserved better.
Like how you agreed
how you dumped me on the driveway, undone and finished
with.
My smile didn't want me.

SOLILOGUIES

Soliloquies of moondust shan't waltz through my window panes
won't shower ribbons of light on the freezing and numb.
They won't save your gracious ache
honest and sincere.
The stars will cradle your grave
and others sprinkle envy on your palms.

But do they know your storms?
Treading lightly on common ground
commercialized in prosperities.

In the morning dawn, where the sheets are warmed
mellow is the dark, where you sing out your defeat

for the rest of the day.
You claim your dignity, your astronomy
where no one else does a doe.

STREET TRASH

I kind of like the look of mess
but I oppose it I digress.

No one ever encouraged me to make something of myself

they only told me I'd be worth it.

The black sheep in the front of the van
mamma's best set of shoes.
Leaving scuff marks in the ruff house of Elvis' blues

setting a light the solitude of the cleaning tools.
They ate without me by the table

how could it be?

THE COLLECTOR

She's the collector
patting down glue into window seal gaps, keeping out the bugs.
Sprinkling music on tapestry
she built it when she was small.

And her body needed work.
Exciting new things to talk about, learn and process.
The boys she could talk about.
Flowers that grew dreadlocks around the smoky thought of dreaming.

She's the lady.
Afraid of nothing, and yet scared of emptiness.

And when it's miserable
when it rains yellow inside of the covers, she'll stay.
Adapting to the fresh sap
honey bees crawling into spaces occupied.

And then she'll wonder her eyes up and down the way you rent
the way you lease, and fold your edges.

In order to find some means of peace.

It's better for her to gather the fluff
then she'll get to the good stuff.
It'll help her sleep
and maybe make the glue stick, if she gets it, just a little bit.
I'm the collector
and you'd never even know it.

THE DANCE

Joint liver rejoice me
one look at you I figure it me.

Why should you perceive me as a maybe
a daydream, a lake scene, a feathered trickled stream.
That is what I am
so may I reduce penalties that fight to keep me in the deep.

Allow me to find the lost pieces
wet
still wet, so I have the possibility to change what I can
and accept what I cannot.

Snake dance, my head dance
that I am always thinking about the chain.

My meaning is clear and its intent.
The heart wanted what they got
never more
never less.

The sweet I rocked to sleep in a serenity that wasn't mine.

I beg to differ.

THE MEANING OF LIFE

All along this fragile way
pebbled with hard sticks and some type of snakes.

In the midst of the never ending fog
there the key lay on my soul.

With every step I took I made sure to run
the ones I was careful to I walked.

And here I was
all this long time.

The answer.

you show up, that's all you have to do to survive.

IN THE MIDDLE

The loom aluminates over me.
A sorrow wall seldom by a reverend telling me he's come to take me home.

Anxiety in my brain glistening over rolled hills.

Guilt.

An investment in my frequent flier.

For I the lonely soul who eats the dark.
Who sees others in the youth of the planetary
and in the age of its contents.

A coil around my heart
the bridge that forces me to get over it.

THIS BODY

The abyss abruptly ruptured the sleep cycle I slept
the moon was full and I smiled to depth.
In tune I can try but the ocean is high and I'm falling
backwards to dive into tahaa blue.
The sky is alive with olive and cold
my body is warming, my hands curve told.
The hair has fluttered from long and beautiful
and my feet are bare with clean cut cuticles.
This is falling with gorgeous layers of circle and I'm trying
to feel the realness of the succumb.
She's feeling tired but she's happy and awake
but the words are manipulating, feeling and moving
changing perception and showing to choosing.
Choose her and choose him but don't pick that one and her
and this.
A life so good may I have just picked so sweet.
Antique of gold, vanity and money.
I have chosen not but to really choose me.
Essence of feet.
So
my scalp is healing and my mind is following,
and here this body is all in it's all.

TROUBLED THINKING

You left me at the cal de sac:

Life support
I asked for life.

Beaten by my own best
imposter at my desk.

It's easy to love
hard to stop.
When you keep falling
keep inviting the calm.

Rest assured I am brave
to be the lioness.

Just that it kills me to know
I am always second place.

I beg you to know
if I'd be happier first.

WE DECLARE A CRY

I am in the in-between of silent writings
birth and soon.
Tonight I waver sleep to dismiss the case of lonesome
slithered in by strangers in their wrong seats.
One heartbreak away from puppy eyes on you.

Wonder wild
your wolf child
you told me I was different and good.

My scars tease me that if being invisible is better than
having to be everything
is it me to accidentally die from it?

In my pride
my angelic shade
do I trip over my own feet?
In my life, answers to seek, under your attitude.
Attached in this nocturnal heart
tether a light to charismatic lust.
Driving through tunnels
a meteorite fell through my clouds.
And everything was still
like Spring sun, August days.

I watch myself from outside of this seat
being washed away with the overflow.
No star wishes
just ashy truths.
The open door turns into tough sleep
reading our conversations over and over.

YOU WROTE TO ME ONCE

Homesick for hands that don't know how to hold mine
like the coffee can on the wooden stove
waiting to be used.

So show me how it would feel to be loved by you!

In the fire of your eyes, the passion in your endless hair.

Like oceans apart
I drift to you through waves like clouds.

My evergreen.
The colour that plays games with me.

I've said your name more than we've greeted
for a cold nose
a less warmer bed.

First of all you'll be my last thought.

Tomorrow's morning face wash

to end this restless windy hollow.

WHISTLE

Punch the horn
and bet on it
because there's no forsaken way swimming lessons taught
me to dive like this.
I don't want to open my eyes
I don't want to see.
Because all's well that ends
and it's a good enough reason for me.

I implore you, eat your initiative, fold it into the forest.
Set aside your goodbye's
like the glint in my opal eyes.

My hopeless habit traces your carnage like milk
fighting a broken faith
as I feel my grip on the rail
and it makes me slip.
By saving myself the trouble it takes to keep my heat
behind its ribcage
and sometimes when I catch myself from a certain angle
I don't think I know me.

Like do all these nights carry a philosophy I'll never truly
get?
When I zero in for the money because I couldn't deal with
boys like them.
I guess I should put guillotine over it
till the two cents stick out.
And I think, maybe this time, but maybe that time
but maybe there's only potential, on this floor of potential.
And if I'm doing it all wrong
I shouldn't be happy about cutting their losses so specially.

HONEY BEE

Peace is the word
and I discovered it within the grazing of your thumbs.

In cinema seats and dimly lit booths
we smiled
and it said everything.

The storm breathed us both out silently
and when I thought I was alone
you kissed my head softly.
Because you speak the loudest as you are
and quickly

I fall harder.
It's reckless to think of you fondly so often as I do
sobriety has tested me yet again.

And I want you more than everything
my best friend
and you're simply the best.

You courted my damaged and other worldly heart as it pondered
a constant duel.
and for the first time, when I was looked at
I felt seen.
Simplicity and elegance brought so much to my new beginning
and it is right for you to have become my passion.

You have ruined me
for I am in love.

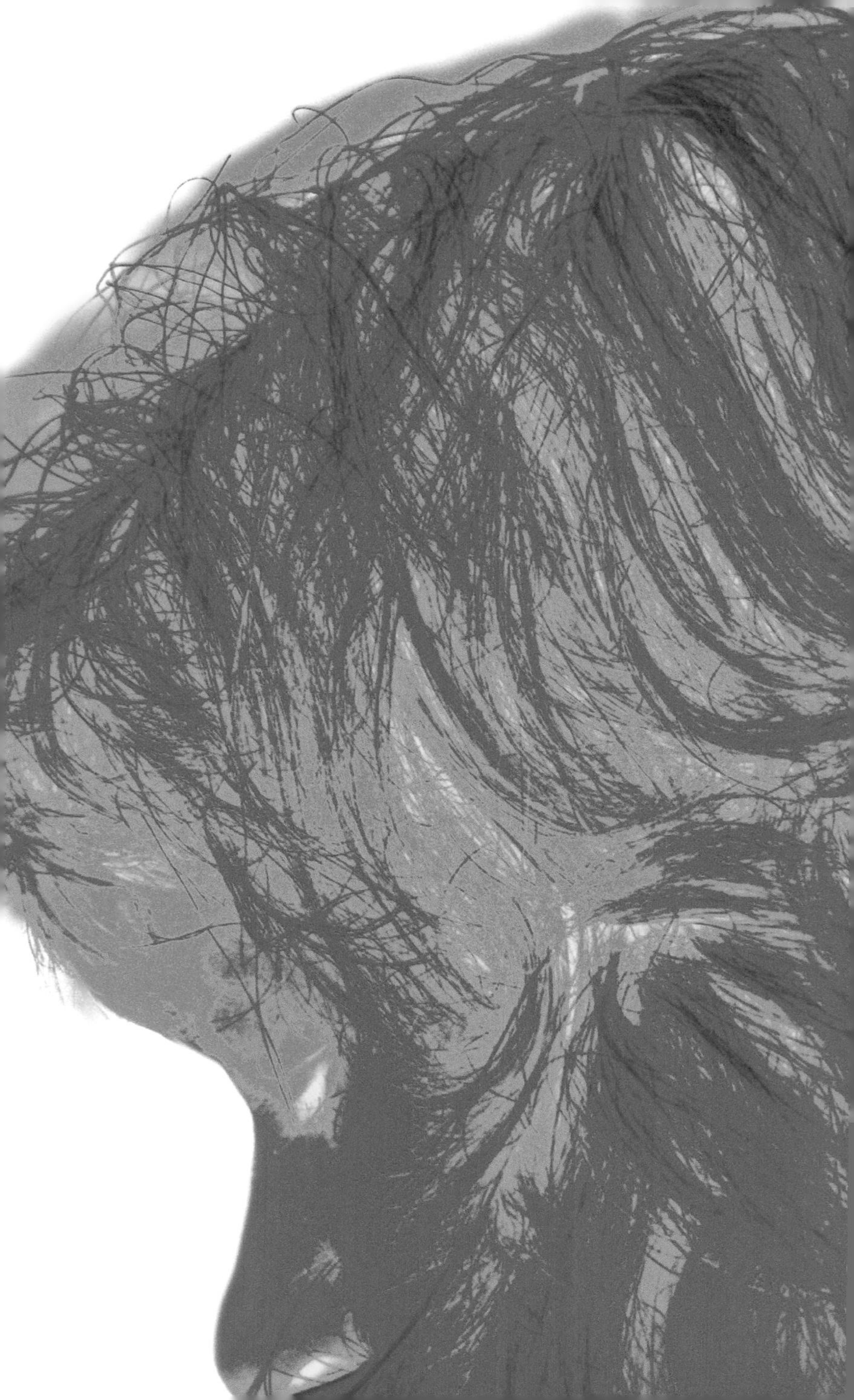

THE ONE

Kick it up

and so you mess it up.

You know I objected to being swept.
As it was
I was used to being stolen from.

So you let me down like we meant nothing
and you pushed me away like a waste of time.
You barked up the wrong tree
and blew things out of proportion.

And cancelled our plans
and denied the gulf between us.

And steadfast my instigations
a wellow away.
That when I finally bit you back for breaking an open heart
I knew damn well
that bad guys dress up as kings.

And when you crossed me on your lonesome
I tickled a thought
I didn't want you round no more.
I visited the breaks, like a bird
allowed a crash from the turn out.

Because I went blonde
and you liked brunettes.

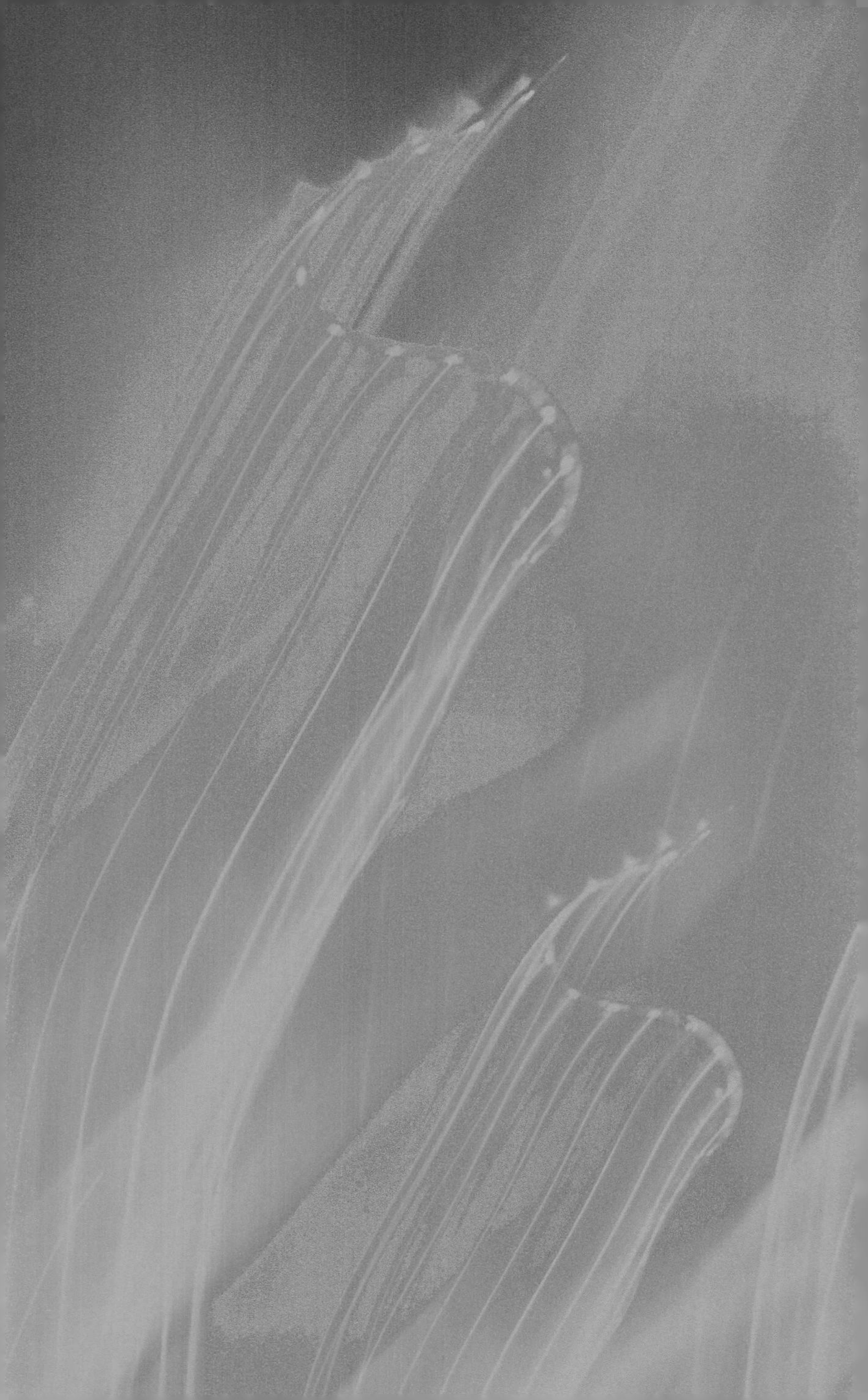

DEPARTMENT 4

Poltergeist on me now
my coping skills digest dealings with a grim reapers of sorts.
If I was internally placid, I would be safe
if I purred suitably, is it impressionable to be heard when I
can't be listened to?
Forgive the way I haunt my past
promise me I will be loved.
I can't reassure my best is good enough
envy sits in a laughable place.
Three feet, it's harder to turn around
sliding foot into the murkiest days.
In this dream I'm suffocating in lards of grease
and when the lights come on, my friends have evaded me.
But it's fine because I don't have much luck with
companionships,
and in order to water them I have to hold them afar.
Yet how is it I've drowned one too many times?
Frankly speaking, I've been stranger than ever
serotonin and dopamine.

TAXI ZONE

Embrace myself as long as this grout dissolved into the cast
iron delays gut feelings.

I think of it in the mornings.
Would he stay, or would he go?

Fold out my calfskin, my pills on the gatekeep.

Will he swallow them all if I let him
would he say goodbye if I let him?

Snakes slither down the hallways on bad days
but the thing is I kiss them just the same.

I was crying whilst running
slicing my sunshine up into getaways.

When world's collied, I never forgot

how I couldn't tolerate my own heart,

when I think of it at night.

JUST

The wind carried up an ultimatum of crick

my car caught its pasture of watery weep.

I called twice, portside no message.

The sky went gloomy, and I bathed in its dysphoria.

Press four, no callback
gotta get my navigation just.

But just I might if I say I like you and all the horses I
tended to through the seasons scamper free

and what if I know it won't work, what if I just.

Because my certainty is that I didn't leave tyre tracks this piety,
but maybe I should?

I can tolerate it, I can softly pass it
so can I; can I sit passenger while you drive me home?

BEDROCK LEMON

My mother was an artist
I caught winds breath that in her past life she was
Rasputin's solider.
Suddenly the hesitation in our army's aperture was
triggered.

The ravens sing kind of loud
the exception of a marsupial spoke, as a feeling of survival
outside her nest.

So I fought em', told em' I could take it
manage the heartache in the distal end of my axons.

But the prophecy manically states she couldn't be saved
the version who's kinship was spoilt with guilt and grief.

Good hell she was just a child
a child in need of notice
ugly duckling.
Foolish of grown ups to suspect anything other than good
intentions

she'll cover my girlhood in a stench I'll never fortify.

NOT JUST A DALLIANCE

I stilled you cobra style, puncturing my oesophagus

rousing an old wife's tale, uncertainty I kept you there.

Pet you through the contention of a pruned veil
alienating my cradle on command
she hurried on.

I untethered notes in margins, on a clouded mind.
Sought salvation; growing among the naked trees
and personified bridges.

There was a Chandler, a Honey and a Peach
in all the men I'd graced before
and then they were names I rolled between my fingers.

In the untouchable, heed by my famine, directly for the love
who's sentencing sat solid on a broken heal.

I laid to rest on his precipice
his simple second heartbeat grave robbed me.

Sleeping dogs lie, when you couldn't look at me
and say yes to everything, hun, I'm just as guilty.
Begotten to bend, lean and bruise fierce
I'm misspent thinking about it, wasted talking about it.
It is better just to live despite it
and with it I go, impossible to forget.

BLONDIE

Don't you know you're kissing the witch?
young donna and the sixty-niner's.

You're the headliners that heal my inner child
my heart bones are in the spirit, behaving in the smoke of the wall's quintessence.

Placed my ego in a pile of destruction
watching my control deteriorate appropriately.

What's appropriate without a quick gas station stop
and the ferocious breeze on your face, when I drive my girls Thelma and Louise rocker style?

I meant what I said
we're going 90's
on hitch.

If you laugh at us you're uninvited
laugh with us, and wild becomes beautiful.

Beautiful becomes powerful
and powerful transitions to enough on the National Highway, A1.

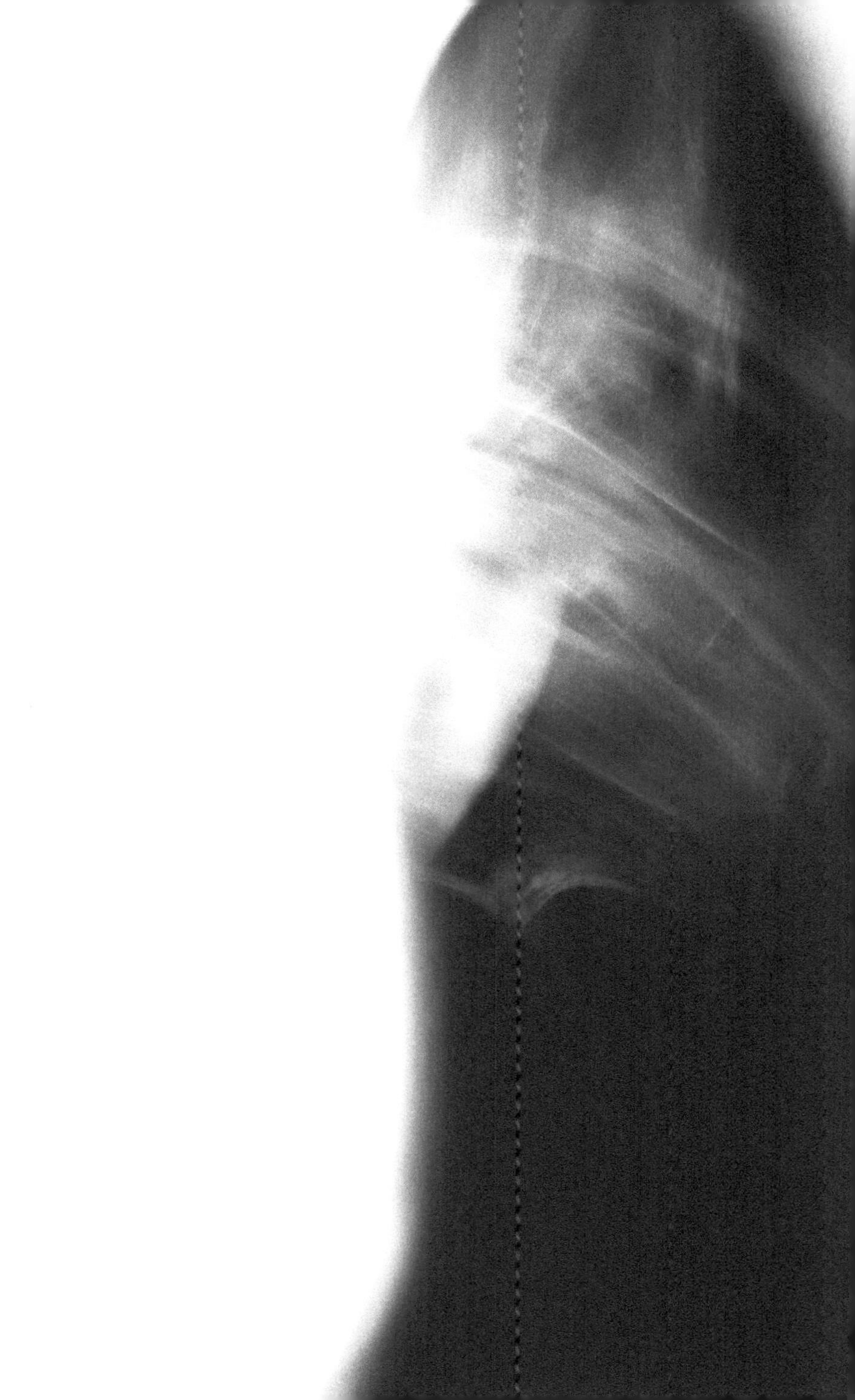

DEAREST INNER CHILD

You are tucked away safely in promises
away from those monsters in your dreams.

Monday when the terror began
I lay by your side to sing to you as you drifted in and out of sleep.

In pink sheets you hid
you broke dread for the night.

I came in the presence of the graveyards you feared.
I was the ghost who protected you when you shut your eyes
from noises made up in your head.
The softness from one pillow was me, who you felt safer within
the friend you imagined sharing strawberry ice cream with.

Took form as the lost you found in the dark
whispered words so you could get better at meeting new people.
Gifted you the courage to settle for second place
but never third.
And made sure you stayed humble
whilst a cruel child took advantage of you in the most conniving ways.
I flew in as ladybugs and fireflies you'd never quite forget
like she was the light from the hallway lamp.
The medicinal in your stomach.
The relief of growing up.
I was you
forever safe,
and I was real. To my inner child,

MoonriderBoots.com

Thank you for supporting an
independent Australian author and publisher.
If you have enjoyed this publication
please consider writing a review via your
favourite online bookstore.

Milton Keynes UK
Ingram Content Group UK Ltd.
UKHW050147280524
443139UK00002BA/2
* 9 7 8 1 7 6 3 5 0 4 9 0 5 *